TOES in my NOSE

AND OTHER POEMS

SHEREE FITCH

illustrations by SYDNEY SMITH

NIMBUS PUBLISHING

Nimbus Publishing Limited
3731 Mackintosh St, Halifax, NS B3K 5A5
(902) 455-4286 nimbus.ca

Printed and bound in China

Cover and interior design: Heather Bryan

Library and Archives Canada Cataloguing in Publication

    Fitch, Sheree
    Toes in my nose and other poems / Sheree Fitch ;
    illustrated by Sydney Smith.

    ISBN 978-1-55109-939-2

I. Smith, Sydney, 1980- II. Title.

PS8561.I86T6 2012   jC811'.54   C2012-903671-4

Toes In My Nose was first published in 1987,
with glorious illustrations by Molly Bobak.

NOVA SCOTIA
Communities, Culture and Heritage

Canada Council Conseil des arts
for the Arts du Canada

Nimbus Publishing acknowledges the financial support for its
publishing activities from the Government of Canada through
the Canada Book Fund (CBF) and the Canada Council for
the Arts, and from the Province of Nova Scotia through the
Department of Communities, Culture and Heritage.

Toes in my Nose

I stuck my toes
In my nose
And I couldn't get them out.
It looked a little strange
And people began to shout

"Why would you ever?
My goodness—I never!"

They got in a terrible snit
"It's simple," I said
As they put me to bed
"I just wanted to see
If they fit."

When Your Sucker Sticks

My sucker stuck to my sweater
My sucker stuck in my hair
Mum had to get the scissors
To cut it out of there.

All because of my sucker
There's a bald spot on my head
To tell the truth
I'd rather have
That sucker stuck instead.

Spreading Honey

How do you get the honey
From the bottle to the bread
Without the bottle slipping
Honey dripping
On your head?

How do you get the honey
From the bread to your tummy?
It's yicky and it's sticky
But it's sweet and it's yummy.

Well, how DO you get the honey
From the bottle to the bread
Without the bottle slipping
Honey dripping
On your head?

You whirl it
You twirl it
You lick it up quick
Then you ask your mommy
For a honey stick.

THAT'S how you get the honey
From the bottle to the bread
Without the bottle slipping
Honey dripping on your head.

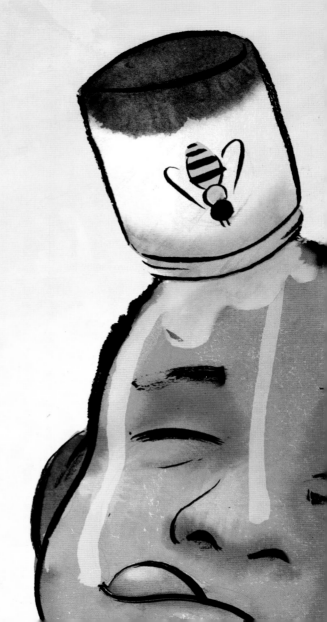

Popcorn Pete

This is the story of Popcorn Peter
Who took all the popcorn
From the movie theatre
He took it home
Hid it under his bed
Then ate and ate
Until his face got red
His cheeks began to puff and swell
What would happen?
No one could tell…
Suddenly there was
This loud KABOOM!

And we all ran up
To Peter's room
Like a piece of popcorn
He **POPPED, POPPED** away
He **POPPED** back into yesterday.

So remember this story
Of Popcorn Pete
And never take more
Than you can eat.

Pocketful of Rocks

A pocketful of rocks
A pocketful of rocks
What do you do
With a pocketful of rocks?

Well, you put those rocks
In your brother's blue socks
And then you watch him walk
With his socks
Full of rocks.

A pocketful of rocks
A pocketful of rocks
That's what you do
With a pocketful of rocks.

Grandmom

My mom's mom is my grandmom
But I just call her Nanny
And Nanny is the neatest granny
Anyone ever had

Nanny knits my mittens
Nanny braids my hair
Nanny smells like violets
Nanny's always there

And Nanny she wears blue jeans
And swings on swings with me
And when I stay at her house
We never watch TV

We look at pictures of my mom
When she was very young
The one I like the best
Is where she's sticking out her tongue

Nanny wears a bracelet
That jingles on her wrist
And whenever Nanny hugs me
She leaves a lipstick kiss

Nanny serves me Kool-aid
In her finest china cup
I'm going to be just like her
Whenever I grow up

When Nanny tucks me in my bed
We play a game of let's pretend
My nanny is my grandmum
My nanny is my friend

And Nanny is the neatest granny
Anyone ever had.

Andrew Oliver

Andrew Oliver Percival Ogilvie
Ordered a pizza with cheese
Pepperoni, bologna and mushrooms
Licorice and lollipops, please
Load on the sauce and the spices
The chocolate-covered ham
Then Andrew preferred
On top of all this
Some strawberry rhubarb jam

Well...

Andrew Oliver Percival Ogilvie
He got indigestion
So next time you order a pizza
I'll give you this suggestion
Order a pizza with cheese
Pepperoni, bologna and ham
But instead of the strawberry rhubarb
Try blueberry rhubarb jam!

Crunching My Lunch

I slurrrp my soup
Upon my spoon
I CRUNCH my crackers up
When I eat my lunch at noon
I b-b-b-blow b-b-b-bubbles in my cup
Now that might not be too polite
But it makes lunch more delicious
It's lots of fun
Until it's time
To clear away the dishes.

The Porcupine

The porcupine is quite divine
She's not so bad at all
But I wouldn't scratch her back
If she came around to call
I wouldn't hug her, either
Though I'm sure she wouldn't mind
I'd never ever sit on her
Or I'd get a sore behind.

But...If that porcupine
Were a friend of mine
I would bring her to my room
That porcupine
Would make a fine
Porcupine
Broom.

Garbage Day

Smash the trash!
Smush it into mush!
Put it on the sidewalk
For the garbage truck.
Watch the men
Throw the bags in the back
Then the trap door closes
And the garbage gets
CRUSHED!

The Watermelon Man

Don't swallow those slippery
Watermelon seeds
Or out of your ears
You'll see that weeds
Are beginning to sprout
And without a doubt
Before you blink
Something green will grow out.

It will dangle from your toes
This long clinging vine
And curl around your knees
Like a thick piece of twine
Over your shoulder
Around your tummy
You'll look like a green
Egyptian mummy!

So chew as carefully
As you can
Or you could become…

THE WATERMELON MAN

William Worm

William Worm
Had quite a squirm
So I picked him up
I kept him for a pet
And put him in a cup.

Then I took him home
So I could show my dad
But for some strange reason
My dad got MAD!

Oh, nooo! he said
A worm! A worm!
A squirmy slimy worm!
Oh, nooo! he said
A worm! A worm!
Worms are full of germs.

But look, I said
Just watch this worm
See how he squiggles?
How he squirms?
His name is William
William Worm
And Bill and I are friends.

Well, William Worm
How do you do?
My father started to grin
I'm sorry to have to tell you, but

YOU CAN'T COME IN!

Now take that worm
With his squiggly squirm
And put him in the ground
That's where worms belong
I cannot have Bill around.

So William Worm
He squirmed away
I looked for him
The other day
I found some worms
But not one squirms
In quite that squiggly way.

The Lizard

A little lizard
Licked his lips
And asked me for
Potato chips
I gave him one
He smiled at me
And ZIP
The chip
Was instantly
GONE
But he wanted more
So I gave him forty cents
And the lizard left for the store.

Mud Mush Dance

I love to squish my toes in mud
Whenever I get the chance
The dirt gets in my toenails
And I do the mud-mush dance—

Mush the mud
Mash the mud
Wiggle your toes in the ground
Squish the mud
Squash the mud
Squiggle the mud around!

I love to squish my toes in mud
Whenever I get the chance
The dirt gets in my toenails
And I do the mud-mush dance—

Mush, squish, squash, splash, mash, mix mud
Squish, squash, mash, mush
Much
Much
Mud!

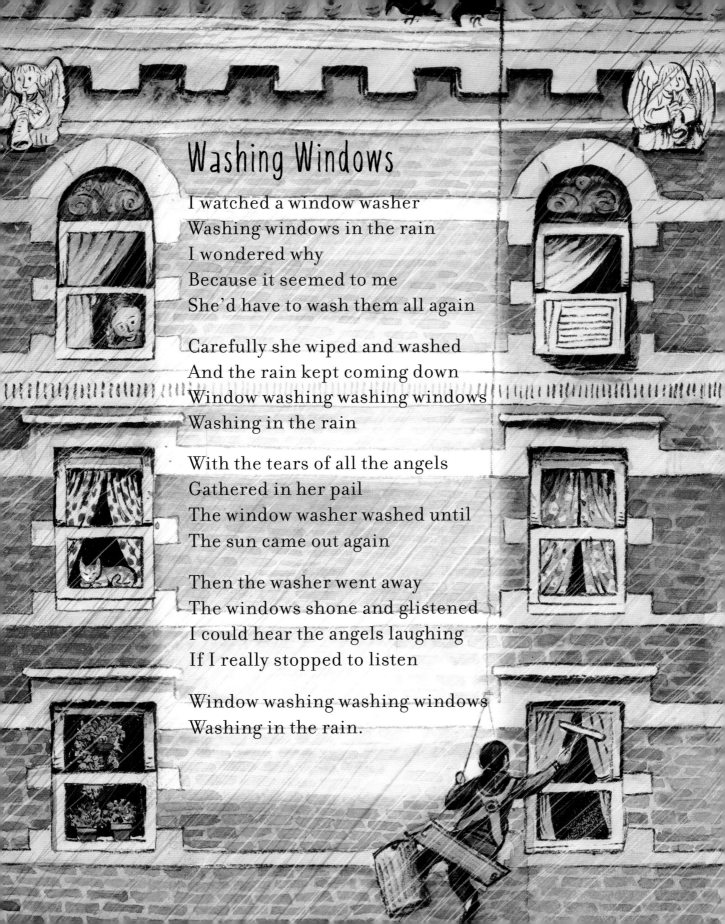

Washing Windows

I watched a window washer
Washing windows in the rain
I wondered why
Because it seemed to me
She'd have to wash them all again

Carefully she wiped and washed
And the rain kept coming down
Window washing washing windows
Washing in the rain

With the tears of all the angels
Gathered in her pail
The window washer washed until
The sun came out again

Then the washer went away
The windows shone and glistened
I could hear the angels laughing
If I really stopped to listen

Window washing washing windows
Washing in the rain.

Doctor Stickles

Dr. Stickles tickled me
And I began to giggle
Dr. Stickles tickled harder
Then I began to wiggle
When Dr. Stickles tickled my toes
I laughed and so would you
Then I tickled Dr. Stickles
Because he was ticklish, too!

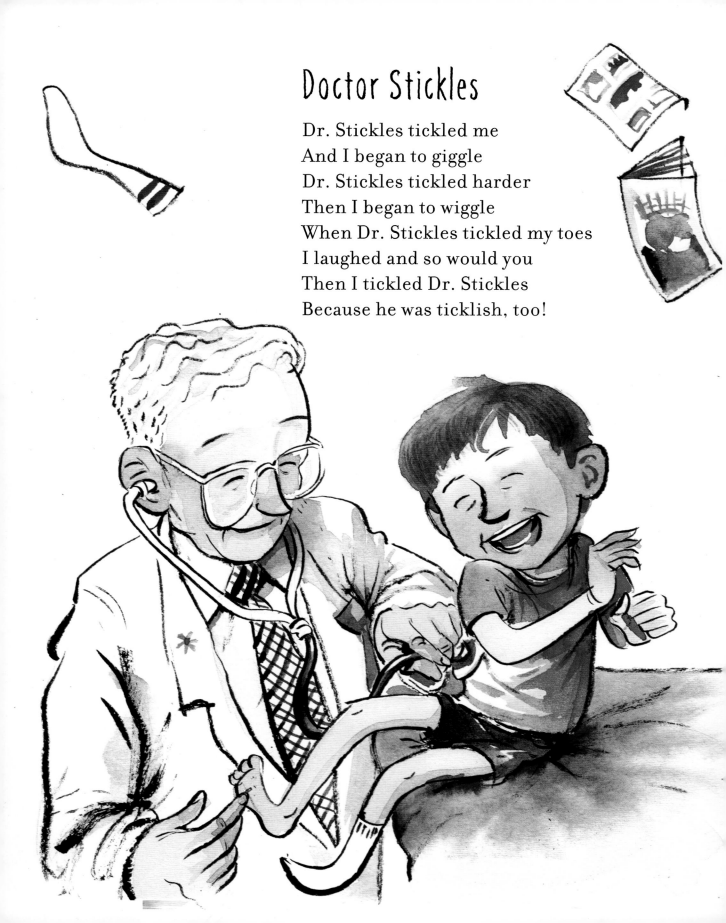

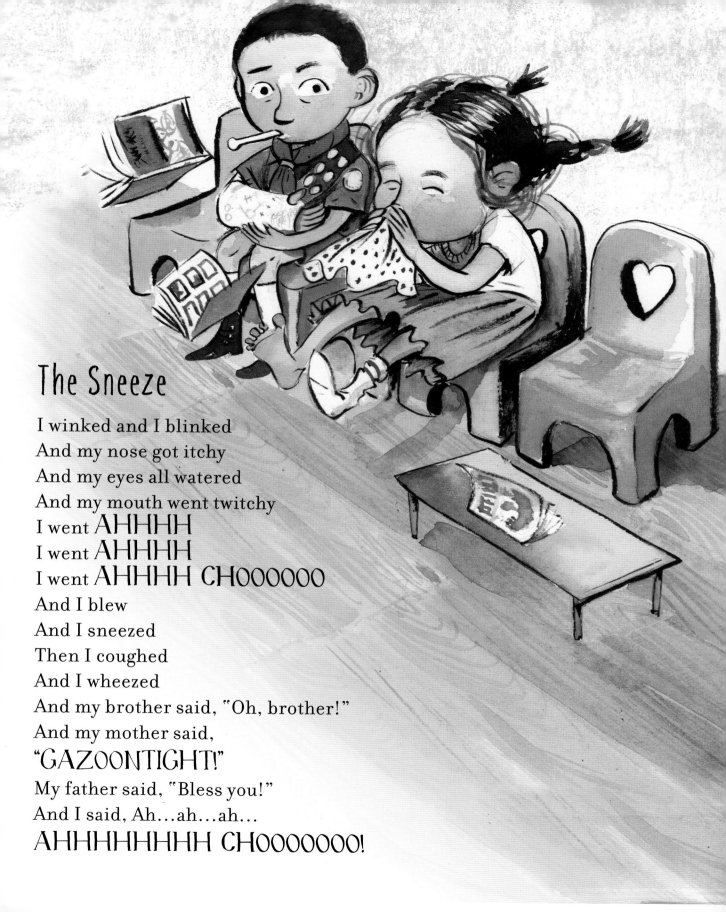

The Sneeze

I winked and I blinked
And my nose got itchy
And my eyes all watered
And my mouth went twitchy
I went AHHHH
I went AHHHH
I went AHHHH CHOOOOOO
And I blew
And I sneezed
Then I coughed
And I wheezed
And my brother said, "Oh, brother!"
And my mother said,
"GAZOONTIGHT!"
My father said, "Bless you!"
And I said, Ah…ah…ah…
AHHHHHHHH CHOOOOOOO!

Mabel Murple

Mabel Murple's house was purple
So was Mabel's hair
Mabel Murple's cat was purple
Purple everywhere.

Mabel Murple's bike was purple
So were Mabel's ears
And when Mabel Murple cried
She cried terrible purple tears.

Zelba Zinnamon

Zelba Zinnamon
She loved cinnamon
She loved cinnamon cake
Zelba Zinnamon
Ate so much cinnamon
She got a belly ache
Then Zelba Zinnamon
Sniffed the cinnamon
Got her nose all red
Zelba Zinnamon
Nose full of cinnamon
Had to go to bed.

Step Away

grocery store
the
to
steps
the
up
more
one
up
then
step
one
up

laundromat
the
to
step
the
up
that
like
just
up
step
one
up

door
bathroom
the
to
steps
the
up
more
one
up
then
step
one
up

place
grandpa's
to
steps
the
up
race
I
up
then
step
one
up

AWAY

step
would
steps
these
wish
I
day
all
step
I
steps
the
up

The Chair

BEWARE!
There's a chair at my daycare
Where you sit if you're caught being bad.
It's no fun
In the chair at my daycare,
In fact, I'm boiling mad.

See, Jeremy Giles, he pushed me,
When no one was able to see.
So I pushed him back
And naturally,
Everyone saw me.

Now Jeremy's eating crackers
And sticking out his tongue,
While I sit here
On this terrible chair,
Wishing I weren't so young.

This chair is full of splinters
It's extremely hard on the bum.
Old Jeremy Giles is having a ball,
And he's blowing bubblegum.

Now they're all playing hide-and-seek,
Jeremy's cheating and taking a peek.
He's having fun—
Just wait till I'm done,
I'll be good for all of next week.

What's that?
My time is up at last?
I'm going to get out of here real fast.
Because Jeremy's taking his place
On the chair
For everyone to see
Now I am good and he is bad,
Or is he as good as me?

My Bouncing Ball

I bounced my ball
And my ball it bounced
Over the house
Over the wall
My ball my ball
It rolled away

I bounced my ball
And it bounced too high
My ball it bounced
Right up to the sky

But…
A ball's gotta bounce
If it's gonna be a ball
A ball's gotta bounce
Or it's not a ball at all

Bounce ball! Bounce ball!
Bounce your ball to city hall!
Bounce ball! Bounce ball!
Over the house!
Over the wall!

But…
A ball's gonna bounce
Cause it's gotta be a ball
A ball's gotta bounce or
IT'S NOT A BALL AT ALL.

Bubblegum Benny

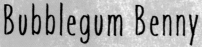

This is the tale of Bubblegum Benny
Who bought some gum
For just under a penny
Now with this gum
He blew and blew
A humungous bubble
It grew and grew
As round as the world
As tall as the sky
And sadly we waved to Benny goodbye
      For the bubble had grown
      Into a big balloon
      And away Benny floated
      Straight to the moon.

The Orangutan

An orangutan rang my doorbell
So I asked him up to tea
The orangutan sat in my kitchen
Then the orangutan sang to me
I banged and twanged my banjo
The orangutan sang his song
We did the orangutan tango
And we diddle-danged all day long
If an orangutan rings your doorbell
Don't call the nearest zoo
Cause the orangutan's quite
A swinger and
He'll sing
His song
For you.

I Wonder About Thunder

I wonder if thunder's
When angels go bowling
If the sky explodes
Because of cannon balls rolling

I wonder if thunder's
A war in the sky
When everyone's angry
But no one knows why

I wonder if thunder's
The burp of the sun
When she's had a big meal
And her supper is done

I wonder if thunder's
Just voices complaining
Because we all know
It's about to start raining

I wonder
About
THUNDER!

The Wind Witch

The Wind Witch comes clattering
Around my back door
With a bang and a battering
With a howl and a roar

She rattles the windows
She steals garbage lids
She blows back the curtains
She loves to scare kids

When the Wind Witch is prowling
The air's full of howling
The whole house shakes with fright
The Wind Witch flies in shadows
And shrieks in the dead of night

I know there's a witch
In the wind when it blows
The Wind Witch is there
When it rains or it snows

The Wind Witch comes clattering
Around my back door
With a bang and a battering
With a howl and a roar.

My Closet

In my closet
In my bedroom
I've got all sorts of things
Like boxes and bags
And bracelets and rings

Whenever I open my closet
Myself
I duck!
Because everything
Falls off the shelf

Marbles and books
All the toys that I own
Papers and pencils
My Lego, a stone
A doll with one eye
A torn teddy bear
His stuffing's all out
His tail isn't there

Feathers and hats
Sneakers and shells
Crayons and paints
  and bicycle bells

More than enough
Of all sorts of stuff
My closet's a crazy place
But that's just fine
Because it's mine
My favourite special space.

Billy's Button

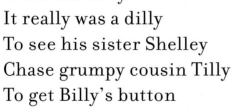

Poor little Billy
Lost the button
From his belly.
Think that sounds
A little silly?
Well, just ask
His sister Shelley.
She knows little Billy
Lost the button
From his belly.
It really was a dilly
To see his sister Shelley
Chase grumpy cousin Tilly
To get Billy's button
Back.
As she stitched it to his belly
Shelley said to Billy,
There you go
You silly willy
Now your belly
Won't be chilly!

Submarine

Splish! Splash!
Splish! Splash!
I am having
My nighttime bath
Daddy scrubs me
Squeaky clean
I pretend
That I'm a submarine.

Underwater
Plug my nose
Signal!
Up the periscope goes
I see a shark
Quick! Get ready!
Hold the boat
Nice and steady.

There it goes
Over there
Oh, no!
I must come up for air
It's time to get out
But that's all right
I'll be back in my sub
Tomorrow night.

The Blug in the Plug

At the end of my bath
When I pull out the plug
There's a monster in the tub
We call
The BLUG

There's a Blug in the plug in the tub
It gurgles and swirls and rumbles
It gobbles up toys
With thunderous noise
And burps and whirls and grumbles

Now this Blug in the plug in the tub
I have never really seen
But I've heard him roar
By the bathroom door
And in the washing machine

The Blug in the plug in the tub
The Blug in the plug in the tub
The Blug in the plug
The Blug in the plug
The Blug in the plug in the tub

Glug, glug, glug, glug, glug...

My Kangaroo

Underneath my bed
There lives a kangaroo
She's been here ever since the day
She left the city zoo.

At night when it is quiet
I climb into her pouch
Then we hop downstairs
    to the living room
We sit upon the couch.

We play a game of checkers
Or sometimes dominoes
Then we stretch up high
We bend and touch our toes.

We hop around the kitchen
To get a bite to eat
My kangaroo likes muffins
Me? I like shredded wheat.

We hop all through the city when
It's very very dark
We hop right past my school
Then we hop down to the park.

Oh, then we slide the slide
And climb the monkey bars
Then we just sit still a while
Gazing at the stars.

And so…we hop back home
And close my bedroom door
My kangaroo is sleepy
And always starts to snore.

I love my kangaroo, and
She loves me, too.
I love my kangaroo

I do…
I do…
I do…

Lola June

On the far side of the moon
Lives a girl named Lola June
And she sings a lullaby
That makes the world go to sleep

Lola June sings her tune
On the far side of the moon

As the stars go sparkling by
With a tear in her eye
Lola June croons her tune
All alone

On the far side of the moon

Getting Out of Getting Into Bed

I'll never understand
Why day turns into night
And I have to go to sleep
And there isn't any light.

Can I have a drink of water?
Then I'll go to bed
My throat is dry without a drink
I'm sure I'll wake up dead.

How about a cracker?
Then I'll go to bed
Better yet, I think I want
A granola bar instead.

Now I have to piddle
Before I go to bed
Well, I wouldn't want a puddle
In the middle of my bed!

To tell the truth
I'd really rather
Stay up late tonight
And paste or paint or colour
Or fly my kite at night
Or…
Rollerskate?
Play hide-and-seek?
Perhaps a pillow fight?

Well, before I go
Just one more thing
My bed is full of bugs
Or maybe we could rock
And have a couple of hugs?

I knew that hugs would work
Now I have to tell you this
I'm really very tired
Here's a goodnight kiss.

Ladder to the Sky

Do you know
If you try
You really can
Touch the sky?

Lean a ladder
Against the moon
And climb, climb high
Talk to the stars
And leave your handprints
All across the sky

Jump on a cloud
And spend the day
Trampoline-jumping
Through the air
Climb a rainbow
And watch the world
From way up there

Then ride that rainbow slide

Back home.

I Can Fly

In my dreams it seems
That I can fly
Very low or very high
Over mountain, over stream
It is my very favourite dream
All night long I swish and swoop
Soar above a silver lake
Until I'm finally tired out
And then I am awake.

The Moon's a Banana

The moon's
A banana
And smiles down at me
With its crooked
Golden grin
Lights up the floor
Of my room
Where the curtain lets it in
Then I don't feel so lonely
With my pillow beneath my head
And the light of the moon beside me
I am happy in my bed.